HOW TO BE A WILDLIFE PHOTOGRAPHER

A magnificent specimen of male Rocky Mountain elk, *Cervus canadensis nelsoni.* Yellowstone National Park in late September. 300 mm. lens, gunstock-mounted camera, Tri-X film, 1/500 sec., f11.

HOW TO BE A WILDLIFE PHOTOGRAPHER

by *Joe Van Wormer*

LODESTAR BOOKS

E. P. Dutton   New York

Photographs not otherwise credited are by Joe Van Wormer.

LIBRARY OF CONGRESS CATALOGING IN PUBLICATION DATA

Van Wormer, Joe.
  How to be a wildlife photographer.

  Summary: An experienced wildlife photographer
explains how to take top-notch photographs of
animals.
    1. Photography of animals—Juvenile literature.
[1. Photography of animals] I. Title.
TR727.V36 1982   778.9'32   82-248
ISBN 0-525-66772-5   AACR2

Published in the United States by E. P. Dutton, Inc., 2 Park Avenue, New York, N.Y. 10016.
Published simultaneously in Canada by Clarke, Irwin & Company Limited, Toronto and Van-
couver.

Editor: Virginia Buckley   Designer: Trish Parcell

Printed in the U.S.A.   First edition

10 9 8 7 6 5 4 3 2 1

To my grandsons Doug, Scott, Erik, and Neal—photographers all

Yellowstone National Park's mighty waterfalls could not compete with this 1½-ounce Yellow Pine chipmunk, *Eutamias amoenus.* 100 mm. lens, Tri-X film, 1/250 sec., f16.

I Possibly the most spectacular scene in Yellowstone National Park is the breathtaking view of the awesome Grand Canyon of the Yellowstone River from Artists' Point. It was the colorfully eroded walls of the canyon—red and brown, but mostly yellow—that gave the park its name. At the head of the canyon roars a 308-foot-high waterfall that becomes a river again in a cloud of rainbow-tinted spray.

On a recent visit to Artists' Point, I walked toward a crowd I thought marked the best canyon viewpoint. I was more than a little surprised to discover that the canyon wasn't even visible from there. Moments later I saw the attraction. A half dozen frisky chipmunks were dashing about the rocks competing for bits of food people tossed to them. The magnificent canyon scenery did not have a chance against this lively sample of park wildlife.

Many of the people were taking pictures of the chipmunks. Undoubtedly, these snapshots will be prized mementos of their trip to Yellowstone, probably much more so than scenic shots of canyons and waterfalls.

There is something unique about a wildlife photo. The animal seems to be alive and in constant motion. 1

The American alligator, *Alligator mississippiensis,* once threatened by hide hunters, now seems to be out of danger of extinction. Photographed in the Aransas National Wildlife Refuge in east Texas. Although they look slow and clumsy, alligators should not be approached too closely. 100 mm. lens, Tri-X film, 1/500 sec., f16.

The chances are that an animal will be different in everyone's snapshot of it, whereas a waterfall looks much the same.

I, too, took pictures of the chipmunks. I already had photos of chipmunks, lots of them. But if there is one thing I've learned in thirty years of wildlife photography, it is never to pass up an opportunity. Probably, with my thousand dollars' worth of equipment and a hundred thousand practice pictures, my shots were better than those of the other park visitors. They should have been, though beginners often come up with excellent photographs. I am certain, though, that those sightseers had just as much fun taking their pictures as I did —and would probably prefer their own, regardless of quality.

Animal stories, animal pictures, and animals in the flesh have always been extremely popular. The growing ecological awareness of recent years has made us realize the hazards of spreading civilization to wilderness areas and animal populations. And an almost daily exposure to good wildlife photography through television, books, and magazines has tremendously increased the interest in wildlife and the photography of it. In any situation where people and wildlife come together, whether it is in the wild, a park, or even a zoo, the number of cameras in evidence is astounding, and so is the number of photographs taken.

Unfortunately, most of the pictures will be rather dull and disappointing, hardly worth a second look. Usually these failures are blamed on lack of "the right equipment" or justified because "I'm just an amateur."

Both are rather lame excuses. Anyone who really wants to make better wildlife pictures can learn do so, 3

A nine-banded armadillo, *Dasypus novemcinctus,* from Aransas National Wildlife Refuge. A voracious insect eater, it can usually be approached quite easily and safely. 200 mm. lens, Tri-X film, 1/500 sec., f16.

After an hour's wait, this mute swan, *Cygnus olor,* brought its bathing and preening to this exuberant conclusion. 300 mm. lens, Tri-X film, 1/1,000 sec., f11.

and within a fairly short time. You may not be able to compete with top professionals in a week—or even in a month or year. But one of the great things about wildlife photography is that you can take pictures while you are learning, see them improve, and enjoy the whole process.

Lack of proper equipment is the poorest excuse in the world for bad pictures. It is true that fine cameras, expensive telephoto lenses, the latest electronic flashes, tripods, and all the other things that a professional carries help him to do his job better. However, this same professional can get good pictures with even the simplest camera. A poor photographer remains a poor photographer regardless of his equipment.

There are always equipment snobs, who look down on anyone with a camera they consider inferior to theirs. The fact that their own pictures are often bad doesn't seem important to them. A professional is more impressed with the way a photographer handles his equipment than with the equipment itself. He generally buys the best he can afford, not because he cannot take good photographs without it, but because with it his job is a little easier.

The greatest asset a wildlife photographer can have is patience. It is the kind of patience that keeps you hidden in a blind for hours, eye on the viewfinder, finger on the shutter release, waiting for just the right combination of light and pose. It may keep you working on the same specimen for days or weeks because you don't want to miss anything important.

5

Not all wildlife photographs need large images of the subject. An osprey, *Pandion haliaetus,* dominates this picture, which gives an effective impression of the bird's home country. 300 mm. lens, Panatomic-X film, 1/250 sec., f11.

A female Roosevelt elk, *Cervus canadensis roosevelti,* greets her three-month-old calf. Story-telling action is well worth waiting for. 300 mm. lens, Tri-X film, 1/500 sec., f11.

Many times I have clicked the shutter when everything looked perfect only to see, moments later, a better or different pose. In that case, I make another exposure. I use a lot of film this way, but I don't miss many pictures. I have often been sorry I didn't take more pictures on a particular occasion; never have I regretted taking too many.

Someone once said that photography is the art of seeing. I agree. Photography not only teaches us to see, it teaches us to see in terms of light and shadow and the effect of both on all the objects within the camera's field of view.

The relationship of these objects forms the "composition" of the picture. We will look into composition more thoroughly a bit later, but don't worry about it. It will take care of itself. Most wildlife photographers compose their pictures without conscious effort, especially when action is involved. They learn to recognize almost instantaneously good composition—or at least the best available to them under the circumstances.

In many wildlife situations, there isn't much time for careful composition. Subsequent study of a photograph may disclose certain weaknesses; but, with wildlife, where you have little, if any, control over the subject, you live with these imperfections. In fact, I have seen wildlife photographs that were so perfect I didn't believe them.

Humor in photography is rare but welcome. This homely young female moose, *Alces alces,* may have been expressing an opinion about wildlife photographers. 200 mm. lens, Tri-X film, 1/250 sec., f8.

The important thing about wildlife photography is to enjoy it. It may lead to nothing more than a pleasant lifetime hobby, or, it might become a useful asset in another profession. It could even turn into a profitable and interesting career in itself.

Never let your fear of making a mistake or wasting film interfere with your fun. Black-and-white 35 mm. film, which most of us start with, is comparatively inexpensive, and we learn from our errors. Often, something we thought looked good through the viewfinder makes a bad picture. But a thorough study of the print should show what went wrong, and a little thought will tell you how to keep it from happening again.

Never be afraid to try something new. Another novice may not agree with your technique, but a veteran asks himself what you may know that he doesn't.

Before going after wildlife photos, an experienced photographer learns all he can about his subject. He wants to know where and when to go to have the best chances for good pictures. He knows how to get close enough to get big images. Even then he constantly reevaluates the situation and changes location or procedures when necessary.

By learning all he can about his subjects, the successful wildlife photographer can recognize the significance of an animal's behavior—whether or not a particular action is typical and meaningful. Ideally, a wildlife photographer should also have some knowledge of zoology or biology—or both. It is not essential, because it is almost impossible not to learn a great deal about animals while you observe and photograph them. Most libraries are well stocked with books about wildlife. A little research before a field trip usually pays dividends. 9

Common snipe, *Capella gallinago,* photographed from a car in the Malheur National Wildlife Refuge in eastern Oregon. 640 mm. lens, Panatomic-X film, 1/250 sec., f11.

Although most people think of cats, dogs, horses, bears, squirrels, et cetera, when they hear the word "animal" the term applies to all living things other than plants—even humans. It is better to be specific—to call them mammals, birds, insects, reptiles, and fish is more accurate.   11

Though definitely an animal, this yellow-bellied marmot, *Marmota flaviventris,* is more accurately described as a "mammal." 100 mm. lens, Plus-X film, 1/250 sec., f16.

Some people don't think of reptiles, such as this iguana, *Iguana iguana*, as animals, but they are. 200 mm. lens, Ilford HP5 film, 1/250 sec., f16.

We call this animal an elk, which would confuse Europeans if it weren't for its scientific name, *Cervus canadensis.* 300 mm. lens, Tri-X film, 1/250 sec., f16.

Each animal species has one or more common names and a scientific name in Latin. Common names may vary from locality to locality, but the scientific name is the same the world over and is accepted internationally.

In this country, for instance, we recognize the moose as the largest member of the deer family. The mature male has great, distinctive, palmated antlers. The scientific name for this animal is *Alces alces.* In Europe it is called elk. However, we have another member of the deer family that we call an elk. It goes by the scientific name of *Cervus canadensis.* All of this would be terribly confusing without the use of the scientific names, which are the same whether we are in America, Sweden, or Australia.

Bird and mammal guidebooks carried by most libraries list both common and scientific names and are often accompanied by illustrations. You won't find any that include all the animals in the world, but books confined to North American species are usually complete and reliable. It isn't necessary to remember all the scientific names; just be sure you know where to find the guidebooks.

I have found it to be helpful, when photographing exotic specimens in zoos and wildlife parks, to note both common and scientific names. These are usually displayed somewhere in the enclosure.

If all this additional knowledge sounds like a burden to acquire, remember, it isn't. In fact, your own desire to know what you have photographed will make it an exciting challenge. One of your greatest pleasures will be to get an outstanding picture and *know* what it is an outstanding picture of.

An Andean goose, *Chloephaga melanoptera,* from the San Diego Zoo Wildlife Park. To be sure of identification, make notes from identifying signs. 200 mm. lens, Tri-X film, 1/500 sec., f16.

16

Unlike the male deer, which has antlers (not horns), which it sheds each year, the bighorn sheep, *Ovis canadensis,* grows only one set of horns during its life (both male and female). 300 mm. lens, Tri-X film, 1/500 sec., f8.

No, this is not a *sneaky* coyote, *Canis latrans.* It is just a coyote being careful, as it and its ancestors have had to be to survive. 300 mm. lens, Tri-X film, 1/500 sec., f16.

Remember, too, that although, scientifically speaking, people are animals, animals are not people. Their actions are mostly instinctive, formed by thousands of years of trying to survive. The fact that they have survived this long is proof that what they do is right for them. You will learn, along with your photography, to evaluate and appreciate animals for what they are and photograph them that way. Don't worry about all the studying you think you have to do. Forget the "have to." Learning these things will follow along with your photography, with little, if any, conscious effort on your part. In fact, you may find that knowing about wildlife is just as enjoyable as knowing about wildlife photography.

Nine-year-old Scott Miles levels his $1 garage-sale camera at the San Diego Zoo's white rhinoceroses, *Ceratotherium simus.*

2 Frequently, someone comes up to me and says, "I'll bet that camera takes good pictures." What I want to say, but don't, is that the camera doesn't take pictures at all. I do!

Equipment performs only as well as the person using it. Too often would-be wildlife photographers do not even get started because they think they do not have the right kind of equipment. The *right* kind is whatever you have. You can learn with the simplest of cameras.

My grandson has a "point-and-shoot" camera he bought at a garage sale for $1. It looks like new and has a built-in flash attachment. On our next trip to the zoo he took several excellent photographs with it; far better, I suspect, than were being taken by some adults we saw using sophisticated cameras that did everything but think.

"Think" is the key word. It makes the difference between good and bad pictures. The kind of equipment most beginners have available forces them to think in order to get high-quality pictures.

Later, after a young photographer has proved his or her ability, it is much easier for him to justify owning 21

With a little help from an enlarger, the point-and-shoot camera
22   produces a creditable portrait.

more expensive equipment, such as a professional or experienced amateur has. The habit of thinking developed while using a simple camera is of inestimable value, no matter how much or what kind of photographic equipment a person will own eventually.

So what kind of camera do you have?

The simplest are point-and-shoot affairs. You load the film, look through the viewfinder, and push the shutter release. There are no adjustments for variations in light; no way to focus; and only a single, fixed shutter speed. This means that this kind of camera should be used only in good light, usually when the sun is shining on your subject. Lenses in these cameras are inexpensive and made so that all objects from near (about five feet) to far (the horizon) will be reasonably sharp.

A subject closer than this "near" distance will be out of focus and blurred. Shutter speeds are fixed at about 1/60 or 1/100 second. Fast-moving objects cannot be stopped with such a slow shutter speed and will usually be fuzzy.

From this basic model camera we move up in price and complexity. Your camera may have an adjustable focus. This can be a footage scale that must be manually set at the estimated distance between lens and subject; or a rangefinder, usually combined with the viewfinder, which brings two images of the subject together when it is in focus; or an image on a ground glass viewing screen that is brought to maximum sharpness by rotating a ring on the lens barrel. Whatever the method involved, the subject should be in focus before the picture is taken. 23

Modern, sophisticated 35 mm. single-lens-reflex camera with all the
controls desirable for wildlife photography.

Advanced cameras have adjustments to control exposure and shutter speed. An iris diaphragm, normally part of the lens system, can be opened and closed like the iris in a human eye. This determines the amount of light that reaches the film.

An adjustable shutter opens for as long as one or more seconds and as short as 1/2,000 second in some instances and controls the length of time in which light reaches the film. In addition to controlling exposure, fast shutter speeds enable photographers to stop motion, such as that of a flying bird or a running deer. At speeds slower than 1/50 second, it is best to have the camera on a tripod. Otherwise, the camera may move, causing blurred images.

The total amount of light reaching the film is determined by both the diaphragm, which controls the amount of light, and the shutter, which controls the time this light is on the film.

Think of this in terms of a water faucet. By opening the faucet (diaphragm) a little or a lot, we can get a trickle or a torrent. The length of time (shutter speed) we leave the faucet on determines the amount (exposure) of water we get. If we only want a gallon (correct exposure), we can open the faucet (diaphragm) to a trickle and get our gallon (correct exposure) in ten minutes (shutter speed). Or we can open the faucet (diaphragm) all the way and get our gallon (correct exposure) in one minute (shutter speed).

Diaphragms are usually marked this way: f4, 5.6, 8, 11, 16, 22, 32. The largest number represents the smallest opening. Each division doubles the amount of light transmitted; that is, f22 passes twice as much light as f32.

Similarly, shutter speeds are usually shown in fractions of seconds, namely: 1/2,000, 1/1,000, 1/500, 1/250, and so on, up to one full second or longer. Some shutters also have a "B" setting, or a "T" setting, or both. "B" means "bulb." When used, the shutter stays open as long as the shutter release is depressed. With the "T" setting, which means "time," the shutter opens when the release is pressed and stays open until it is pressed again. Exposures of many seconds, minutes, or even hours can be obtained this way.

Consequently, correct exposure can be any one of several combinations:

1/25 second at f32
1/50 second at f22
1/100 second at f16
1/200 second at f11
1/400 second at f8
1/800 second at f5.6
1/1,600 second at f4

All give the same exposure. Some cameras may not have these exact shutter speeds. In that case, use the nearest —for example, 1/500 for 1/400, or 1/1,000 for 1/800. The variation will not be enough to affect the exposure noticeably.

There are reasons for using a particular combination of diaphragm setting and shutter speed, but we need not concern ourselves with them at this time. As your skills develop, you can refine your technique. For now, if you have a camera with controls, keep your shutter speed at 1/100 second and the diaphragm setting at whatever goes with that shutter speed under the prevailing light conditions.

This Portland, Oregon, Zoo lion and cub, *Panthera leo,* are obviously in an enclosure, but the cub looking at its father makes a better-than-average picture. 200 mm. lens, Plus-X film, 1/250 sec., f16.

If, however, you are using a *fast* film (we will discuss film speed later), use a shutter speed equal to the film speed. For instance, for ASA 400 film, use 1/400 second.

So how do you tell what that diaphragm setting should be?

With each roll of film there is usually included an instruction sheet. It shows shutter speed and diaphragm settings for that film under various light conditions, such as bright sun, cloudy-bright, heavy overcast, and open shade. I suggest that you make a practice of studying thoroughly all instructions, especially for a film you're unfamiliar with or a new piece of equipment. Read them carefully several times.

Another method of determining correct exposure is with photoelectric exposure meters. They react either to light reflected from the object to be photographed or to light falling on the object. The first is called a reflective meter; the second, an incidence meter. Some are both. In either case, light causes a needle to move across a calibrated dial in proportion to its strength. By scales on the meter, the correct exposure or, more accurately, several correct exposures, can be read.

Reflected-light meters must be used with care in order that only light reflected from the principal subject is measured, rather than, for instance, the intense light of a clear sky. Shade the meter with your hand to prevent this. If necessary, take a reading from some nearby object the same color as your subject that has the same light falling on it.

An additional complication is the "speed" of the film. Different films have different sensitivities to light. They are tested and assigned ratings in accordance with established standards to indicate their sensitivity.   27

Film speeds are represented by such numbers as ASA 100, ASA 50, et cetera. A film rated at ASA 100 is twice as fast as one rated ASA 50. When using simple cameras with no exposure adjustments, be sure to use film recommended for that camera. With cameras that have electronic exposure controls and photoelectric exposure meters, film speed is taken into account by setting the ASA number on a built-in dial.

At the beginning it is best to avoid unnecessary complications. Choose one black-and-white film and stay with it. For a simple camera, use what the manufacturer recommends, or, if the recommendation is for a foreign-made film, get an American-made film with the same ASA rating. If your camera has exposure adjustments, choose a film of medium speed, such as ASA 100. Color film is more expensive than black-and-white. Since you will use a lot of film, leave color alone until you have learned all you can from black-and-white.

After you have used a certain film for a while, you know what to expect from it under most light conditions.

I've been making serious wildlife photographs for many years, but I use only three different films: one medium-speed color, one slow black-and-white, and one fast black-and-white. I'm usually too concerned about what I'm seeing through the viewfinder and whether or not I'm getting something good to worry about which of a dozen kinds of film is in the camera.

Many newer cameras have built-in exposure meters by which the exposure can be adjusted while looking through the viewfinder. Some go even farther and have an automatic exposure that requires only an initial setting of the film speed along with either the shutter speed or the diaphragm. In a few models, it is only necessary to set the speed of the film. The camera does the rest. This sounds better than it is. So much automation does not allow the photographer certain controls, such as shutter speed, he may want to use.

Most beginners do their learning with simple, inexpensive cameras, but some may have access to better equipment. The good wildlife photographers that I know mostly use 35 mm. single-lens-reflex cameras. There is a wide price range in this type of camera, and quality basically goes along with cost.

The single-lens-reflex gets its name from the fact that the subject is viewed through the taking lens. Light from the subject enters the lens, strikes a mirror and is reflected upward onto a ground glass and through a prism. The photographer looks into the viewfinder toward the subject and sees exactly what the camera sees in an upright image in correct left-to-right position. The ground glass image is brought into focus by rotating a ring on the lens barrel.

These cameras are excellent for wildlife photography. Light and compact, they provide easy lens interchangeability. Most of them are made in Japan, and even the least expensive ones should give many years of good service if they are not abused. If you can afford such an outfit, by all means get it. If you can't, don't be discouraged. You can learn to be a good wildlife photographer without it, even though your range of subject matter may be more restricted.

A comparatively recent addition to the lineup of inexpensive cameras is a model using 110 film. Negatives from 110 are only about one fourth the size of full-frame 35 mm., and prints suffer accordingly in en-

Nine-year-old Erik Skorpen aims his "used" range-finder camera at the Denver Zoo's black-tailed prairie dogs, *Cynomys ludovicianus,* with excellent results.

largements. However, this is not much of a drawback unless very large prints are desired. Smaller prints, 3½" × 5", for example, are adequate to judge the quality of your photography. Many manufacturers offer these small cameras. Here, too, price indicates quality. Film comes in plastic "drop-in" cartridges that are generally notched to indicate film speed. In some advanced camera models these notches activate exposure controls within the camera, so exposures will be correct for that film.

Some models convert from a normal lens to a telephoto by moving an auxiliary lens over the normal lens. This is valuable to a wildlife photographer even though the telephoto effect gives a negative image only 1½–2 times the size of an image from a normal lens.

If you are planning to buy a camera, don't overlook used ones. Unless a camera is mistreated, it does not wear out easily. Besides, the constant appearance of new models on the market often makes available older ones in excellent condition at bargain prices. Compare prices and insist on a trial period before buying. Get permission to have the camera checked by a reliable camera repair shop. Most importantly, buy from a reputable dealer. He will not knowingly sell you a bad camera, as he makes most of his money from selling film and other supplies.

Holding the camera properly to avoid movement at the moment of exposure is one of the most important requirements for sharp pictures.

PHOTO BY ALLAN SKORPEN

So now you have your camera and are anxious to load up with film and get started. Don't do it yet! Take plenty of time to familiarize yourself with the camera. Be sure you know how to load and unload it. You would be amazed at the number of camera owners who don't. Handle it until it feels comfortable. Practice holding it rock steady in picture-taking position. More photographs are spoiled by camera movement than by any other single cause.

Each style of camera requires a slightly different hold. Basically, a camera should be held with both hands and pressed firmly against the face. Keep your elbows in close to your sides for additional stability. Brace yourself against a solid support whenever possible.

When what you see through the viewfinder is what you want in your picture, press the shutter release firmly. Do not jab it, poke it, or punch it. *Firmly press it.* You can tell when you've done it correctly: there is no movement noticeable through the viewfinder when the shutter releases. Practice this until it becomes a habit. Also, follow through by holding the camera in shooting position for a half second or so after the shutter releases. Otherwise, there may be a tendency to move the camera before exposure is actually completed, and this would, of course, result in a blurred picture.

Cameras using 110 film are rather thin and flat. They are harder to hold steady than more conventionally shaped cameras. Also, because the shutter release is on one end, the camera is easily moved during the instant of exposure. Put your forefinger on the shutter release, your thumb underneath it on the bottom of the camera, and pinch them together. This equalizes pressure at the top and bottom of the camera. 33

Gray wolf, *Canis lupus,* at the Olympic Game Farm in Washington.
34   200 mm. lens, Tri-X film, 1/500 sec., f11. <small>PHOTO BY DOUGLAS EDWARD MILES</small>

Regardless of what camera you have, it pays to take care of it. Small camel's hair brushes for removing dust should be used carefully both inside and out at frequent intervals; whenever changing film, if possible, but always when a photo session is over or if you've been using the camera under dusty conditions.

Be extra careful when cleaning the lens, the most important part of your camera. Brush it gently with lens tissue torn in half, or with your brush. Do not rub the lens to clean it. Any grit present can scratch the surface. Should you get a fingerprint on it, a drop of liquid lens cleaner and the careful use of lens tissue will remove it. But avoid this kind of lens cleaning whenever possible.

A carrying case is good camera protection, but you may wish to leave it behind during actual photography sessions. Some cases are always in the way when the camera is in use. However, a neck or wrist strap may keep you from dropping the equipment.

Never store cameras or film in the glove compartment of a car. During warm weather this is like putting them into a heated oven. Heat quickly spoils film. Avoid dusty spots. If dust is bad and your camera is not in a dust-proof case, put it in a plastic bag.

Water, especially salt water, can be death to a camera and bad for most other kinds of photo equipment. Complete immersion is often ruinous. A little rain isn't quite so bad, but try to avoid it. In any event, dry the camera as quickly as possible, inside and out. Never put it away wet, and if you think moisture got into the mechanism, get it to the repairman as soon as possible. 35

Cleanliness is a must all the way from loading the camera to making the print, especially when working with 35 mm. and smaller negatives. A tiny piece of grit can scratch a negative or transparency. When enlarged, the scratch becomes an unsightly blemish.

The average wildlife photographer makes many negatives and must protect them from dust, scratches, and fingerprints while he studies them. There are plastic negative holders that can handle thirty-five or thirty-six negatives. They help to keep negatives clean and are highly recommended.

3 Before you start taking photographs in earnest, you should have some idea as to what makes a good picture. There are really two kinds of "goodness" to strive for in a photograph: technical excellence and pictorial quality.

The first—technical excellence—means good exposure and sharpness. This is easy.

Proper exposure comes automatically with some cameras, which have built-in photoelectric measurement; with others, it is easily achieved by using an exposure chart or by separate photoelectric exposure-meter readings.

Sharpness results from holding the camera motionless during exposure after carefully focusing on the main subject; or, in simple, nonfocusing cameras, by keeping the subject within the fixed zone of focus. Most point-and-shoot or fixed-focus cameras give their best results when the subject is between five and twelve feet away. Theoretically, focus extends all the way to infinity, but in practice the image deteriorates when the subject is too far away.

The most difficult thing to achieve is pictorial quality —whatever it is about the picture that arouses the ob- 37

This photograph of mute swans, *Cygnus olor,* has compositional short-comings, but it tells a story, which more or less compensates for any weaknesses. 400 mm. lens, Tri-X film, 1/500 sec., f16.

server's interest. A photograph that has nothing to offer except that it is well exposed and sharp isn't much. But one that grips the viewer's attention, even though it may not be completely sharp or perfectly exposed, can be very good.

When a photograph is sharp, well exposed, *and* emotionally stirring, it may well be exceptional.

Most "good" pictures—good, that is, from the standpoint of their emotional content—are well composed. Composition—the arrangement of the various elements within the picture—is a matter that is endlessly debated and is subject to constant disagreement even among experienced photographers, who know exactly what it is but often have great difficulties describing it.

Composition will drive you crazy if you let it. Don't! In the first place, *good* composition is nothing more or less than a pleasing arrangement of all the elements in a picture. The key word is *all*. It takes a lot of time and experience to learn to see and recognize all the elements. The natural tendency is for the eye to see only the main subject and ignore backgrounds, masses of light and dark on the sides, telephone poles, scraps of paper on the ground, et cetera. It pays to practice looking through the viewfinder and consciously picking out other things besides the principal subject. Eventually, this becomes more or less automatic, and unwanted objects are eliminated by moving around to change the camera's viewpoint.

There are three points I usually observe to improve my pictures: get closer; get action; and use a filter (a yellow filter for black-and-white film, a "skylight filter" for color.

Close-up of a young female Roosevelt elk, *Cervus canadensis roosevelti,* is packed with action and interest, with no distracting elements. 200 40 mm. lens, Tri-X film, 1/500 sec., f11.

Recently, I was photographing birds in the Tropical America aviary in the San Diego Zoo Wildlife Park. A brilliant orange-colored male Cock-of-the-Rock flew down to the edge of a small pond for a drink. I was across the pond from this bird, with no way to get closer. I checked the scene through the 200 mm. lens I was using and gave up. The bird was too small to dominate the composition.

Standing alongside me was a young man who didn't agree and proceeded to take several pictures through his normal lens. I'm sure he will wonder what happened to the bird when he sees his prints. It will be just an orange spot he'll have to describe rather than a picture that speaks for itself.

Many photographers seem to have trouble judging how close to their subject they really are. Practice on your cat or a chicken or a horse. Look at your subject through the viewfinder. Move closer until the edge of the picture finally cuts into your subject. Now you're getting a full-frame photo. Notice how close you are. How does it compare with the distances from which you usually shoot close-ups? Practice this until you are constantly aware of how close you really are and how large an image you are going to get. You won't want to take all your photographs at this distance, but at least you will know what your picture will look like when you're really close.

But, you might ask, what do you do when you can't get closer? Wait around. The subject may eventually move. Otherwise, forget it and move on. There is little point in wasting film.

Startling action, such as this bounding mule deer buck, *Odocoileus hemionus,* with all four feet in the air, always makes a photograph more interesting. 300 mm. lens, gunstock-mounted camera, Tri-X film, 1/1,000 sec., f11.

An exuberantly racing coyote, *Canis latrans.* 200 mm. lens, Tri-X film, 1/500 sec., f16.

Action makes a photograph more interesting. This does not necessarily mean physical action, such as running, jumping, or flying. It can also mean implied or pictorial action (like a look, for instance) or a potential action. A lion crouched ready to attack or a deer alerted to approaching danger is not in motion, but the action is there in the tenseness of the pose.

There should always be room in the picture area for the action to take place, or, at least, to get started. Leave some room on the side toward which the action is directed. And if the action is (or is about to be) on a diagonal line, so much the better. Diagonal lines of action appear more energetic.

43

A yellow filter darkened the sky and added dramatic impact to this picture of a flying western Canada goose, *Branta canadensis moffitti.* 135 mm. lens, 2× yellow filter, Plus-X film, 1/250 sec., f11.

44

Filters are also used to improve picture quality. Usually made of colored optical glass, they can be used in front of or behind the lens. They permit light of the same color as the filter to pass through to the film, while screening out other colors.

There are many different kinds of filters for both color and black-and-white film. Their use sounds complicated, and it is, in its ultimate refinement. For our purpose, though, we can keep it simple. We'll consider only two filters, a 2× yellow for black-and-white film, and a skylight filter for color.

The "2×" designation means that we must double the exposure because the filter allows only half the normal amount of light to pass through. The effect is to darken blue skies that would otherwise show in our print as white or light gray. Such dark skies add dramatic impact to your photographs. Without a lot of blue sky in the picture, the yellow filter has little value.

With cameras that have no exposure adjustments, using such filters would underexpose the picture, with the exception of some of the 110 cameras previously described. Their shutter speeds can be reduced by the insertion of a spent flash cube or FlipFlash, which lets you pick up enough additional exposure to offset that lost by the filter. A word of caution: When reducing the shutter speed in this manner, take extra care to hold the camera motionless during exposure.

The skylight filter removes much of the ultraviolet light, which has a tendency to give a bluish cast to color pictures, especially in shadowed areas. The filter has no effect on black-and-white film and does not require an exposure increase. Furthermore, it protects the lens from dirt, scratches, and fingerprints. I have one for each lens and leave them attached all the time.

Burchell's zebra, *Equus burchellii,* photographed in Kenya, Africa. The picture would be better without the distracting segment of another zebra at the right rear, but to capture this fleeting "smile," it was necessary to shoot fast. From a Kodachrome transparency. 300 mm. lens, gunstock-mounted camera, 1/250 sec., f8.

As you work at your craft, study your negatives and prints. Look at the pictures of fellow photographers and discuss your work with them. Study photos in books and magazines. If you like a photograph, try to see all the things in the print that make it effective. If you don't like it, try to understand why not. How would you have done it better?

Your tastes will gradually change. You will become more and more critical of your own work and that of others. Your sense of composition will sharpen. Your judgment will improve. If you're lucky, you'll become your own toughest critic. You can improve your photographs only when you learn to be a severe judge of your own work. I have never taken a picture that I did not feel could have been better.

A free-roaming, semitame bobcat, *Lynx rufus.* A lot of waiting and walking produced this unusual drinking picture. 300 mm. lens, gunstock-mounted camera, Tri-X film, 1/500 sec., f16.

Golden-mantled ground squirrel, *Citellus lateralis,* with its cheek
pouches full of food, provides an amusing story-telling photograph.
640 mm. lens, Tri-X film, 1/250 sec., f22.

Raccoon, *Procyon lotor,* a pet, looks fierce posing for its portrait. 100 mm. lens, Tri-X film, 1/250 sec., f16. Wait for the subject to turn its head so you can see a catchlight in its eyes.

50

Sarus crane, *Grus antigone,* a native of Asia, was photographed in an Oregon drive-through wildlife park. 200 mm. lens, Tri-X film, 1/500 sec., f16. PHOTO BY DOUGLAS EDWARD MILES 51

A five-month-old white-tailed deer, *Odocoileus virginianus.* Center of interest is at one of the one-third points. 300 mm. lens, gunstock-mounted camera, Tri-X film, 1/250 second, f11.

Eventually, someone will mention the "rules" of composition. I do not care for that term. It seems to put composition into a mathematical category, as if certain exact placements would automatically ensure success. Actually, the human eye always looks for balance in a picture, which is produced by a certain arrangement of its various elements. Someone decided to study pictures until he was able to recognize certain patterns in these arrangements, which he then reduced to "rules." A few of these rules are worth noting simply because knowing them saves time in learning to recognize good composition in your own photographs.

Many wildlife photographs as well as scenic pictures have a horizon line in them. The natural tendency when taking a picture is to place this in the center. But experience has taught that this is monotonous. It is more pleasing to have the horizon line one third of the way up from the bottom or one third of the way down from the top.

This one-third division is important in the placement of the center of interest that all good photographs have. The eye does not like to wander all over the place looking for something important, and there seem to be certain areas to which the eye is attracted first.

Take a rectangular piece of paper, approximately the dimensions of a photographic print, and draw lines on it that divide it into thirds both vertically and horizontally. There will be four points where lines cross. These are the approximate points that attract the eye and where the center of interest of the photograph should be located. Which point one uses is generally determined by the subject matter and its relation to other objects in the photograph.

Yellow-bellied marmot, *Marmota flaviventris*. 640 mm. lens, Tri-X film,
1/250 sec., f22.

In wildlife photography, as in the photography of people, the subject's eyes are most important. They are usually the center of interest and should be placed at one of the one-third points. Which one to select depends on the direction in which the animal is looking, for there should be room within the picture for this action. If it is, in effect, looking out of the picture, the viewer may be disturbed by not knowing what it sees.

One should always try for a catchlight in the subject's eyes. This is a reflection in the pupils that gives a feeling of life. It is visible in the viewfinder whenever the subject is close to the camera. Some photographers may add a catchlight by using a weak flash. The artificial light, in such cases, is not enough to affect the exposure, but it does put a highlight in the subject's eyes. 55

Simple pictures are effective, such as of this serene-looking avocet. Good separation between subject and background is essential. 300 mm. lens, gunstock-mounted camera, Plus-X film, 1/250 sec., f16.

Put light-colored subjects against dark backgrounds and dark-colored objects against light backgrounds. A viewer's eyes are attracted to light objects, and any large, unimportant light area will draw attention away from the center of interest. Always try for angles that eliminate or subdue such distractions.

Do not hesitate to try different viewpoints—high, low, and in between. Move from one side to another and observe how this shifts objects around in the viewfinder. A low angle, such as you might get by lying on the ground, will often raise your subject and avoid an otherwise unsightly background. Likewise, a high viewpoint, as from a stepladder, can change the entire appearance of a shot. Wildlife subjects seen from unusual angles are frequently very intriguing. Water-level shots of ducks or geese, for example, give us completely different views of the birds from the ones we usually see from above.

A family of western Canada geese, *Branta canadensis moffitti,* framed by
58 trees. Normal lens, Panatomic-X film, 1/250 sec., f11.

Often dark objects in the picture, such as trees, rocks, or bushes, can be used as a frame. This directs the viewer's eye to the center of interest and holds it there. Such framing is a very effective tool in making a picture more interesting. I have, on occasion, carried along a leafy branch and had someone hold it so that it protruded into the picture area to provide framing. This technique can also be used to fill up the corner of an otherwise empty sky.

Photograph made to emphasize the distinctive ears of a black-tailed
jack rabbit, *Lepus californicus.* 300 mm. lens, Tri-X film, 1/500 sec., f16.

Each photograph you take, if it is to be any good at all, should have a reason for being. Why do you want the picture? If you have no reason, you will have no real picture—only wasted film. The more precisely you are able to recognize what you want in a particular shot, or what there is about the scene that interests you, the better your chances of getting a good one.

For example, if all you want is a picture of a lion, it is only a matter of pointing a camera at the lion and clicking the shutter. At best, all you will have is a record. But, if you have in mind a shot that shows the dignity and power that has earned this animal the title King of Beasts, you may have to work and wait until you capture that through the viewfinder. 61

The golden-mantled ground squirrel, *Citellus lateralis,* is a handsome and friendly little fellow. 100 mm. lens, Panatomic-X film, 1/250 sec., f11.

The high horizon line is desirable in this typical head-low pose of a male Rocky Mountain elk, *Cervus canadensis nelsoni,* approaching a female during the mating season. 640 mm. lens, beanbag support from a car, Tri-X film, 1/500 sec., f16.

Even in Africa, lions, *Panthera leo,* spend most of their time asleep,
which makes for dull pictures. This fierce-looking expression is really
only a lazy yawn. 300 mm. lens, gunstock-mounted camera, 1/250
sec., f8, copied from Kodachrome transparencies.

If you study the animal further, you may begin to notice other things that interest and even excite you. The lion might yawn, displaying that great open expanse of powerful jaw with its double row of lethal-looking teeth. It's a picture you must have!

Perhaps the relationship between a mother lion and her cubs intrigues you. You wait for interaction between mother and young. Animals doing something are nearly always more interesting than animals asleep or just resting. Shoot them eating, scratching, yawning, fighting, running, or playing. Watch for good expressions. Fear, interest, surprise, aggression, or curiosity sometimes show on an animal's face.

A black-tailed prairie dog, *Cynomys ludovicianus,* nibbles daintily a tasty
blade of grass. 640 mm. lens, Tri-X film, 1/250 sec., f22.

When you begin to think in these precise terms and eliminate that which does not contribute to your main purpose, your pictures will get better.

You might merely want an identification picture of some animal. This is a perfectly legitimate reason, and when approached with that specific purpose in mind, you're likely to get a good one. A well-lighted shot of a rare okapi, standing more or less broadside to the camera with all four feet showing, may not be as exciting as other poses you might get, but it shows all the identifying features of this unique animal. Later you might want a shot of one showing its unbelievably long tongue reaching for a mouthful of succulent leaves or some other pose that emphasizes its unique characteristics. 67

Luck is helpful, but be ready to take advantage of it. Young rare kit fox, *Vulpes velox,* photographed from one of Nevada's main highways. 600 mm. lens, Tri-X film, 1/500 sec., f11.

Roosevelt elk, *Cervus canadensis roosevelti.* Photograph made to show part-albino yearling male, just right of center. 200 mm. lens, Tri-X film, 1/250 sec., f11.

The angle at which light hits your center of interest affects the pictorial value of the photograph. Generally, early-morning and late-afternoon light are more pleasing than the bright glare of the noonday sun. However, never pass up an otherwise good photo opportunity simply because it is lunchtime. Nearly every picture has a shortcoming or two. That noontime shot may be worthwhile despite the overhead lighting.

Many simple cameras have no adjustments to compensate for hazy sunlight, cloudy days, or subjects in the shade. In this case, pass up taking pictures where the light is not good. If your camera does have adjustments for poor light conditions, some beautiful effects can be obtained without heavy shadows or strong light.

Many of the available 110 point-and-shoot cameras have flashbulb features for use when the light is too poor for normal photography. When the flash cube, or FlipFlash attachment, is inserted in the camera, the normal shutter speed of around 1/100 second is automatically changed to about 1/50 second. (There are a few exceptions. Some cameras a single fixed-shutter speed of about 1/50 second.) This, in effect, doubles the exposure. Consequently, under dim light conditions, such as open shade, a used flash cube or FlipFlash can be inserted to obtain the lower shutter speed and get twice the normal exposure of the shadowed subject. 69

Side lighting often increases the impact of a photograph. Mule deer
fawn, *Odocoileus hemionus.* Twin-lens reflex, normal lens, Tri-X film,
1/250 sec., f11.

Since actions and expressions of wildlife are unpredictable, you should always be ready for the unexpected. It often provides those rare and unusual photographs we all admire. But once you have taken such a picture, be ready for another. What follows may be even better.

Film is comparatively inexpensive, and it is much easier to discard a dozen mediocre negatives than it is to recapture a lost chance at something really great. It is always a good rule to shoot the best picture you can and then try for a better one.

But although I am a strong advocate of making many exposures, this doesn't mean that you should print all of the negatives. It is possible to have only negatives developed and to choose the picture to be printed after studying them. Better yet, have a contact sheet made.

Always be ready for the unusual, whether in the wild, a zoo, or a
72   park. 200 mm. lens, Tri-X film, 1/250 sec., f16.

This is a single (usually 8″ × 10″) print upon which all the negatives from a single roll have been contact-printed. This print may seem expensive, but it is only a fraction of the cost of even small enlargements of all the negatives. With a magnifying glass, contact prints can be studied and evaluated and the best selected for enlargement.

I suggest that anyone seriously interested in photography learn to process and print his or her own negatives. It is not difficult, and learning the rudiments does not take long. To become an expert is not quite that easy, but skills grow with experience. Since darkroom work is really a separate subject, we won't pursue it further here. But I do hope you will try it. 73

The formula for a good dog picture is not much different from the one employed to get a good coyote picture. 100 mm. lens, Ilford HP5 film, 1/500 sec., f16.

Locating and getting within range of a coyote, *Canis latrans,* may be difficult, but once accomplished, it is much like photographing a large dog. 200 mm. lens, Panatomic-X film, 1/250 sec., f11.

4 Before tackling wildlife subjects, practice a bit on domestic animals. If you can't take a good picture of a dog or cat, where things are pretty much under your control, you have little chance with coyotes and cougars. Simply because the subject matter is unusual to you does not guarantee that your pictures will be good. If you've ever tried to get a good picture of your or someone else's favorite animal, you'll know how frustrating it can be. But all the requirements for good wildlife photographs still apply.

In almost every locality there are dogs, cats, parrots, and parrakeets to practice on. Occasionally, you may find an unusual pet that is really a challenge. Besides, any pet owner appreciates good pictures of his animal.

I have photographed such odd pets as marmots, badgers, bobcats, black bears, skunks, deer, pronghorns, owls, hawks, and a white leghorn rooster that liked coffee. I've listened to magpies that talked, cuddled a porcupine, and gone hiking with a coyote with a sense of humor. It was all great fun. I made many satisfying pictures and learned a lot of things. One of them is to be cautious around once-wild animals, especially pets that have lost all fear of people.

Photographs of domestic cats, such as this mixed-up shot with legs going in all directions, will test your ability to get an interesting picture. 100 mm. lens, Ilford HP5 film, 1/500 sec., f16.

Or you may get a chance to unlimber your lens in Africa on a rare ground shot of a leopard, *Panthera pardus.* 300 mm. lens, 1/250 sec., f8, copy of Kodachrome transparency.

With plenty of practice on various cats, you should be ready to photograph a bobcat, *Lynx rufus,* in the wild. 200 mm. lens, Tri-X film, 1/250 sec., f16.

It is difficult to get a bad picture with this kind of subject matter.
78   Normal lens, electronic flash, Tri-X film, f16, twin-lens reflex camera.

A handsome, well-trained Arabian stallion. Horse people are proud of their animals and appreciate good pictures of them. Range-finder camera, normal lens, Tri-X film, 1/1,000 sec., f16.

For practice on larger animals, try a farm. I doubt that many farmers or ranchers would deny you permission to photograph their stock. When you can get good pictures of cows and horses, you can take good pictures of the larger hoofed wild animals. A horse at a hundred feet gives you about the same size image as an elk at that distance and you'll soon learn how close you need to be to wild animals that size to get a big image.

Taking pictures of sheep and pigs will teach you how to photograph smaller hoofed animals. There are usually chickens on a farm, often ducks and turkeys, frequently pigeons, and always a quota of cats and dogs. Try them all.

Mallard hens, *Anas platyrhynchos.* Luck plays a part in shots like this, but practice on pigeons sharpens your reflexes. 200 mm. lens, Tri-X film, 1/500 sec., f16.

With domestic animals, as with wild animals, backgrounds should not detract from the center of interest. You need good lighting and composition, and, if you can catch them, interesting actions or expressions.

One important thing farm photography allows you to do is to practice getting close to large animals for those desired, frame-filling images. Although some farm animals might be dangerous, such as a cantankerous old bull or a belligerent ram or billy goat, most are mild mannered. The farmer can tell you which ones to beware of.

Getting close to wild animals is a photographer's greatest problem. Tiny images are not very interesting. The professional or advanced amateur may have hundreds, even thousands, of dollars invested in telephoto lenses, the sole purpose of which is to produce large images without the necessity of getting close to his subject.

Generally, an animal in the wild tolerates the approach of a person only so close before it moves away. This distance varies with individual animals, seasons, and other conditions. Seldom is it short enough to give the wanted large image with a normal or short telephoto lens. Ideally, the photographer gets as close as he can and then uses a telephoto to bring the image up to the size he wants.

There are other reasons for using a telephoto, however. In cases where an animal might be dangerous, the photographer should stay a safe distance away, even though the animal might tolerate a closer approach. At other times, he might wish to remain at a distance so as not to influence an animal's actions and thus get truer photographs of its activities.

There is a definite similarity between photographing a proud white
leghorn rooster and a giant Canada goose, *Branta canadensis maxima*.
Rooster was photographed with normal lens, Plus-X film, 1/250 sec.,
f16. Goose (opposite page) was photographed with 300 mm. lens,
82   Tri-X film, 1/500 sec., f16.

In the beginning, most of you will not have much in the way of telephoto equipment. So how are you going to get close enough to wild animals to get good pictures? You go to the zoo!

Wildebeest, *Connochaetes taurinus,* play fighting. There is nothing in the picture to indicate that it was made in the San Diego Zoo. 200 mm. lens, Ilford HP5 film, 1/500 sec., f16.

In today's zoos, the animals are so near that a long telephoto lens is not always necessary. Even a modest one—85 mm. to 200 mm., for a 35 mm. camera—will often give dramatic close-ups. If you have one, use it. However, we are concerned mostly with the problems faced by the majority of beginners who may be equipped, at best, with a point-and-shoot camera having a built-in telephoto converter. Most of your pictures will be taken with the telephoto lens. Except for the larger mammals, one is seldom close enough to fill the frame with the subject through a normal lens.

Of course, zoo photography is not quite the same as wildlife photography in the field, but it is similar enough to provide excellent training and great satisfaction. It also gives you an opportunity to photograph exotic specimens you may never see in the wild. In fact, there are some so rare or elusive that the only way they can be photographed is in captivity.

Also, believe it or not, it is often more difficult to get a good picture in a zoo than in the wild. Backgrounds, foregrounds, even the surface upon which an animal stands or lies may look artificial. The photographer has little opportunity to find more suitable viewpoints. Fortunately, the trend now is to exhibit animals in open grottoes with simulated natural backgrounds. Deep moats effectively keep the animals confined.

In the wild any picture of an animal is authentic. In zoos, you are faced not only with getting the animal in an interesting pose or action, but with eliminating all signs that might show the picture was made in a zoo.

It is not considered ethical to claim wild and natural settings for zoo pictures, but there is no reason why you can't make them look that way, if possible.

Spot-nosed monkey, *Cercopithecus nictitans,* photographed through
88   wire. 100 mm. lens, Ilford HP5 film, 1/500 sec., f16.

A zoo has something else in its favor: It is available all year long and most zoos encourage photographers. The San Diego Zoo, one of the finest in the world, will even lend you a simple camera without charge. However, there may be photographic restrictions in some zoos, and it is best to learn what they are before starting.

The best time of day for zoo photography is early morning, when it is generally cooler and the animals are more active. They are also apt to be hungry and moving about in anticipation of feeding time. The slanting rays of early-morning light are more interesting than those at midday. Besides, you are ahead of the crowds which, unfortunately, often show little regard for a serious photographer. I have had people squeeze in front of me just as I was about to take a picture I'd been waiting for all morning.

The next-best time is from midafternoon on to closing time, during which many of the animals will have another activity period.

The worst time is midday. It is often hot. The animals have usually been fed and are apt to be lying down or standing around half asleep.

Early morning and later afternoon are also the best times to photograph in the wild. During the middle of the day few wild animals are about and active. I have been in Yellowstone National Park at sunrise when elk were everywhere. Three hours later you couldn't find one.

Some seasons are also better than others. Because of the crowds, summer-vacation time can be bad. Spring and autumn are probably the best. Where winters are severe, many animals are moved into warm enclosures.

As you grow familiar with "your" zoo, you'll learn what specimens are active at what times.

Changing one's viewpoint only slightly will often eliminate obvious signs of the zoo. 100 mm. lens, Ilford HP5 film, 1/500 sec., f16.

Most zoos are connected in some way with a companion zoological society. If there is a zoo nearby, a membership in this society has much to recommend it, especially if the usually modest yearly fee permits members to visit the zoo anytime during normal open hours without additional payment. Monthly bulletins often inform members of new animals on exhibit and the birth of young. Frequently, special programs may be arranged for members only.

However, being a member of a zoological society does not entitle you to special privileges in and around animal enclosures. You should be extremely conscientious about obeying the rules, such as staying behind restraining walls or fences. This can be most frustrating when being a few feet closer would let you shoot between the bars at a spectacular snow leopard, for example. But being a few feet closer might also permit the leopard to reach through and get a photographer.

Film boxes, wrappings, and used flashbulbs should go into the nearest trash barrel or your pocket. The least you can do is to take care of your own garbage.

As photographer at the zoo you are not a privileged person. Other visitors have as much right there as you do. Most of them will respect your efforts if you don't hold them up too long. However, there are always some who do not mind scaring the animal you're working on. There's nothing you can do about that but be patient.

In a zoo there are often bars, wires, or glass partitions between your lens and the animal you are photographing; on the other hand, you don't have to travel ten thousand miles, face unpredictable weather, or invest thousands of dollars in telephoto lenses, blinds, and other equipment.

Portrait of a muntjac, or Chinese deer, *Muntiacus muntjak,* made in the entrance aviary of the San Diego Zoo Wildlife Park. 100 mm. lens, Ilford HP5 film, 1/250 sec., f5.6.

Wire, glass, brick, or other man-made backgrounds present difficulties, but not insurmountable ones. Some fencing of the chain-link type has openings of an inch and a half or so between the wires. The camera can be placed in one of them to center the lens. Bars or fencing with smaller openings can be blurred into disappearing altogether by placing the camera directly against the barrier; although you should avoid having a bar directly in front of the lens. Also, don't do this if there is a dangerous animal on the other side. With long telephoto lenses, bars can be blurred out of the way even at a distance, as can the background, by setting the camera's diaphragm on the largest opening the light conditions and available shutter speed will permit and still give correct exposure.

With point-and-shoot cameras there is little you can do with bad backgrounds other than to look for a viewpoint where they won't show. Sometimes heavy shadows will effectively hide the background if the subject is brightly lighted.

Glass is troublesome at best. The photographer must guard against unwanted reflections, loss of light, and, with simple cameras, a subject too close to be in focus. Reflections come from light sources over which you have no control as well as from your own flash unit. Those from outside sources can be eliminated by having someone shade the glass with a black cloth; reflections from your own light, by shooting at an angle to the glass.

Some light is lost through the glass, but an exposure correction of about one half f-stop should take care of it. Some trial photographs will help establish the necessary exposure adjustment. Glass is seldom as clean as it

Crowned pigeon, *Goura cristata,* San Diego Zoo Wildlife Park aviary.
94   100 mm. lens, Ilford HP5 film, 1/500 sec., f11.

should be. A can of glass cleaner and a clean cloth can solve that problem, but it might be wise to ask the keeper if he minds.

However, in most modern zoos, there are many areas where these problems do not exist. In addition to the previously mentioned grottoes, there are walk-in aviaries where visitors and animals, usually birds, more or less mingle in a suitably landscaped enclosure. Some aviaries can be wire-walled bird cages, some as big as a barn, or solid-walled and roofed structures.

Waterfowl ponds are often wide open right to the water's edge. Zoo waterfowl are generally pinioned (having the outer joint of one wing removed) to prevent them from flying. They become quite tame and, seen against a neutral background of water, often provide striking pictures. Always try to get the unpinioned side of the bird toward the camera.

In some aviaries, especially those inside buildings, the light may be so poor as to make photography without flash virtually impossible. So far as I know, all modern cameras have some form of built-in flash contact. Flashbulbs, electronic flash—or both—can be used for dim-light photography.

Even when the zoo background is obvious, it can be minimized with effective presentation of the subject. Big brown, or Kodiak, bear, *Ursus middendorffi.* 200 mm. lens, Tri-X film, 1/500 sec., f16.

96

Flash has a limited effective range. In simple cameras this may be no more than ten feet, so they must be used reasonably close. An electronic flash is generally better for animal photography than flashbulbs. The duration of the flash is much shorter and consequently less annoying. In most instances, electronic flash will be completely ignored by the animals, especially after a shot or two.

After the initial investment, which is not prohibitive, electronic flash is quite inexpensive, costing only a cent or so per picture. Many companies offer basic models that are quite reliable. Exposure is determined by the distance between flash and subject and the speed of the film. A calculating dial on the flash unit makes exposure determination simple.

Light in any particular part of the zoo varies during the day as the sun moves around. After repeated visits, you'll soon learn, for example, that the sun hits the lions at 9 A.M.; the ducks at ten; but elephants are in the shade until after lunch. Before long, light characteristics for the entire zoo will become familiar to you. These gradually change, of course, with the seasons.

Wait a while. Maybe your sleepy tiger, *Panthera tigris,* will wake up
and give you a good shot. 300 mm. lens, Tri-X film, 1/500 sec., f16.

Animals, whether in the wild or in a zoo, are not always cooperative. In a zoo, however, you can always work on other subjects and then come back. If the tiger is asleep when you arrive, it does no good to yell at him. He's been yelled at so often he ignores it. Don't, under any circumstances, throw anything at him. Such an action will most likely get you tossed out of the zoo. Nor should you attempt to arouse the tiger with an offering of food. Most zoos now forbid the feeding of animals.

Animals that are alert often pace restlessly about their enclosures. This is not necessarily because they're unhappy and want to get out. It is more probable that they feel the need of exercise. A few moments' observation will disclose any pattern to their movement and indicate desirable picture situations. With limited equipment, this is often the point at which the animal is nearest the camera.

Most animals look better at certain times of the year. Mammals shed their winter fur during spring and summer and in the process may look like a bundle of old rags. Birds lose old feathers and grow new ones, and look bad during the replacement period. Some even have different plumage during different seasons. Mammals generally look their best in late fall and winter; birds, just before nesting begins. Zoo keepers can tell you when the animals are in prime condition.

It is impossible to photograph any modern zoo in one day—or even one month, for that matter. To try is to guarantee disappointment. Of course, one can run through, making snapshots of each enclosure, but all you are apt to have for your efforts is wasted film. Take your time, try to get above-average pictures of whatever you can cover in your allotted time, and come back.   99

There is little to show that this black bear, *Euarctos americanus,* was photographed in the drive-through section of the Olympic Game Farm in northwestern Washington. 200 mm. lens, Tri-X film, 1/500 sec., f16.

PHOTO BY DOUGLAS EDWARD MILES

The comparatively recent establishment of drive-through wildlife parks provides interesting new possibilities for the wildlife photographer who hasn't the time or opportunity to visit faraway places. These parks are, as far as I know, all privately owned, and the admission fee is fairly high. However, there is generally no time limit, and one can stay inside all day. Photography here is similar to that in the wild, with the only restrictions being that you must stay in your car; the car must be kept on the roads; and, in carnivore areas, all windows must stay closed.

All the animals are fenced in, but the compounds are usually so large that fences do not intrude on backgrounds or are easily avoided. Long telephotos are useful, but the photographer with minimum equipment can do well if he is willing to wait while a desired subject wanders into range. A good wildlife photograph does not depend on the remoteness of the location, the dangers involved, or the rareness of the subject. It can be made almost anywhere there are animals if the photographer is skillful.

Free-roaming wild turkey, *Meleagris gallopavo,* at Northwest Trek, a wildlife park. 200 mm. lens, Tri-X film, 1/500 sec., f16.

PHOTO BY DOUGLAS EDWARD MILES

A handsome male black buck, *Antilope cervicapra,* a native of India, alive and alert in an Oregon drive-through wildlife park. 200 mm. lens, Tri-X film, 1/500 sec., f16.　　PHOTO BY DOUGLAS EDWARD MILES　103

Typical lineup of cameras and lenses from one of Japan's manufacturers of quality 35 mm. single-lens-reflex cameras.

5 Regardless of what kind of camera a wildlife photographer starts with, he will, eventually, want a single-lens-reflex (SLR) and a telephoto lens or two. Although some use SLRs that take pictures 2¼" × 2¼" or slightly larger, the majority depend on 35 mm. SLRs. There is a reason for this. The larger cameras are quite expensive, and I've found them to be heavier and slower to use. Also, there is a somewhat limited number of makes and models to choose from.

On the other hand, 35 mm. SLRs are available from a great many manufacturers in an elaborate array of models, prices, and features. Furthermore, new models come along so fast that dealers frequently find themselves with obsolete merchandise on hand. Often these cameras can be purchased at great savings, as can others, slightly used but still good, that have been taken in trade.

There is also a large selection of telephoto lenses for 35 mm. SLRs in a wide range of prices. The best lenses for any given camera are quite likely those made by the manufacturer for that specific camera, but they may also be the most expensive. There are quite a few indepen- 105

These three pictures show the effect of different focal-length lenses.
Made at the San Diego Zoo Wildlife Park within minutes of each
other and all from the same viewpoint, they show a group of Grant's
gazelles, *Gazella granti*. No. 1, normal 50 mm. lens. No. 2, 200 mm.
106   lens. No. 3, 650 mm. lens. Ilford HP5 film, 1/500 sec., f16.

dent lens manufacturers who offer telephotos for nearly all SLRs. Their lenses are surprisingly good and usually somewhat less costly than those made by the big-name companies. However, quality may not be consistent and one should always insist on the right to try one and return it if not satisfactory.

Choosing one with the right focal length is not easy. No single lens covers all situations. Experienced wildlife photographers carry several.

Lenses are described by their focal length and largest aperture. Focal length is the distance from the center of the lens to the film when focused on infinity. This distance is expressed in either millimeters or inches. A 50 mm. f2.0 lens has a focal length of 50 mm. (about 2 inches) and a maximum diaphragm opening of f2.0. In 35 mm. photography, a 50 mm. lens is considered normal. Anything longer than that is a telephoto. A 200 mm. lens is four times as long and produces an image four times the size of that of the normal lens. To put it another way, you will get the same-size image at twenty feet with a 200 mm. lens that you do with the 50 mm. lens at five feet.

Telephotos are available in many focal lengths. Some are over 1,000 mm. and so large that it takes two tripods to hold them steady. The question you face, of course, is how large a lens should you get? Large telephotos are, in general, more expensive, but that isn't their only drawback. Size and weight make them slow and difficult to handle. Maximum f-stops are usually smaller, requiring longer exposures; consequently pictures are more susceptible to subject and camera motion. A telephoto that magnifies the subject six times will also magnify camera motion six times.

A tripod or some other form of support with long telephotos is a must
if sharp pictures are to result.

We generally think of telephotos as being long and tubelike, but today there are quite a few telephotos that are not long at all, but short and fat. These are catadioptric lenses, a combination of focusing mirrors and conventional glass lenses. Instead of light going straight through the lens, as it does in the usual telephoto, it is reflected and focused within the lens barrel a couple of times. As a result, a 750 mm. (30-inch) lens may only be 10 inches or so in length.

Catadioptric lenses have some drawbacks, of course. They have fixed apertures. The good ones are expensive. Out-of-focus background highlights are doughnut-shaped, which is not always desirable. Conventional telephotos are, I believe, better for the beginner.

A good rule to follow is to use the shortest lens that gives the image size you want. In other words, if you are near enough to fill the frame with a 100 mm. lens, use it. Don't put on a 300 mm. and back off. As a rule, the shorter the lens, the better the picture quality.

In my work, I use five telephoto lenses varying from 100 mm. to 650 mm. Probably 95 percent of all my wildlife photography in the field is done with a 300 mm. In zoos and wildlife parks the 200 mm. takes over. The 650 mm. is used mostly from blinds, where the subjects are small birds. The 200 mm. is normally hand-held with a shutter speed of at least 1/125 second, although I prefer 1/250 or 1/500. The 300 mm. is hand-holdable, but I am not comfortable unless I have it on a gunstock arrangement to provide both steadiness and flexibility. The 400 mm., an in-between spare, and the 650 mm. are always used on a tripod or beanbag.

One of the main features of SLRs is the fact that previewing the picture and focusing is done through the 109

taking lens. The most modern of them use a truly re-
markable bit of optical engineering called a fully automatic lens.

With this lens the aperture is preset. Focusing and
viewing are accomplished with the lens wide open.
When the shutter release is pressed, several things hap-
pen in literally the blink of an eye:

(1) The aperture closes down to the preselected setting.
(2) The reflecting mirror flips up out of the way.
(3) The shutter exposes the film.
(4) The aperture returns to its largest opening.
(5) The mirror drops down into viewing position.

A fairly recent development in telephotos is the zoom
lens. It is described as 100 mm.–300 mm., for example.
This means that by adjustments on the lens barrel, the
focal length can be anything between 100 mm. and 300
mm.—210 mm., for instance. The lenses are heavy and
expensive and, unless well made, do not produce pictures as sharp as their single-focal-length counterparts.
They do have the advantage of eliminating the need to
carry several lenses, as well as saving the time that
might otherwise be lost in changing from one lens to
another.

Various focal-length combinations are available: 75
mm.–150 mm.; 70 mm.–210 mm.; 90 mm.–230 mm.; 100
mm.–300 mm.; et cetera. If I were chosing a zoom lens,
I would look for between 90 mm. and 100 mm. on the
short end and between 250 mm. and 300 mm. on the
long end. I would also get the best I could find. Even
though it might be quite expensive, the chances are that

it would not cost as much as the several lenses it replaces.

Although all lenses are capable of focusing on infinity—objects very far away, each has a limitation on its close-up focusing. This can vary from 18 inches in normal lenses to forty or more feet in very long lenses. Frequently, one wants to focus closer than the lens will permit. The near-focus limit can be extended by use of extension tubes or a bellows. Both are mounted between lens and camera. However, it is impossible to focus on distant objects when these items are in place.

Another comparatively recent development for SLRs is the tele-converter or tele-extender. This optical instrument looks much like an extension tube with a lens in it. It is mounted between lens and camera and makes a longer telephoto out of the one you are using. With a 2× converter, a 200 mm. lens becomes a 400 mm. one; a 600 becomes a 1,200, et cetera.

As with most optical "magic," there are drawbacks to tele-converters. Some might not be up to the quality of your lens, with a resultant loss of image quality. *All* lower the effective aperture of your lens—a 2× by two stops; a 3× by 3 stops. I favor a lens without a converter except under emergency conditions.

Many wildlife photographers waste their time and money searching for a miracle telephoto. There is no such thing! It is far better to have one good, medium lens, 300mm., for example, and learn to use it, than to own a half dozen assorted lengths you haven't mastered.

A friendly young American robin, *Turdus migratorius,* with a little more angleworm than it could handle, was photographed at close range with a normal lens and a short extension tube. Tri-X film, 1/250 sec., f16.

6 There are two general methods by which wildlife photographers in the field get close to their subjects—by stalking and by using blinds, which the English call "hides."

But there are exceptions to these methods. A few years back, while on location on the fringes of the central Oregon desert, I sat on a pine log fifteen feet from a tiny waterhole and made full-frame pictures all day of what seemed like an endless variety of birds. I was in full view but moved as little as possible even when reloading the camera. Several of the birds were so trusting that they perched on the telephoto lens while I was taking pictures.

Unfortunately, such situations cannot be counted upon. Normally, considerable advance planning—and the use of blinds—is required. Blinds are most commonly used for birds. They can, at times, be used for mammals, although mammals are usually suspicious of a blind near their waterholes or dens. Human scent sticks to blind material, and it is almost impossible to position one so that it is always downwind from subjects.

You can get started using blinds at home, as there are birds almost everywhere. Even in densely populated metropolitan areas there are sparrows or starlings, and always pigeons. A seed feeder in the yard near a window or on a window ledge in an apartment should attract whatever birds are in the neighborhood. They soon learn to expect the food and become quite tolerant of people.

Use the house as a blind and close off a window with a sheet of cardboard or plywood. Close-up pictures can be made through a hole in this screen without disturbing the birds. I once had a most successful blind of this type made by cutting a lens-sized hole in a window shade. When not in use, the shade was rolled up out of the way.

Food to interest the different bird species in your locality should be included in your feeding program— wild bird seed for seed eaters and beef suet for insect eaters. Peanut butter mixed with cornmeal or rolled oat flakes is enjoyed by many species. Sugar water in suitable feeders attracts hummingbirds. House finches and hooded orioles have also used my hummingbird feeder.

Most species do not like to fly directly to a feeder, preferring, instead, to stop short and look over the situation first. A suitable perch for this "caution" stop, placed for maximum pictorial effectiveness, may be the best spot for pictures.

It is helpful to make feeders look like something else. A small log or limb with holes bored in it to hold food works fine. But anything that will make the food container look natural will do. Camera viewpoints can usually be lowered enough to keep the food containers from showing in the picture.

Backgrounds should not conflict with the intent of
114 the picture. For black-and-white film, a medium-to-

light-gray background will probably be most satisfactory. For color, blue sky or green foliage often works well. Under some circumstances a piece of plywood painted light blue or green may be used to cover up an otherwise unsightly background. These "backdrops" can also be used for black-and-white photography, as they print as a light or medium gray.

For use in the wild, blinds can be made of almost anything that conceals the photographer—canvas, burlap, wood, logs, brush. Small tents make very good blinds. Canvas or other cloth should be stretched tight to avoid flapping in the wind and frightening the subjects. The blind should have an opening for the camera lens and peepholes at the front and sides, so activities around the blind can be observed. It should be large enough to hold the photographer, his camera equipment, including tripod, a comfortable folding chair, canteen, and, probably, lunch. One three feet square and four feet high is roomy enough for one photographer.

Always enter a blind expecting to stay several hours, or even all day. The chair, water, and food keep discomfort at a minimum. I often take a book with me in case there are long periods of waiting.

Place blinds near spots where birds are known to be present. Nests are favorites, as are waterholes and feeding stations. Take care to locate the blind so that the light strikes the subject at a favorable angle. The distance between blind and subject is determined by the length of telephoto one expects to use; or, if you have a selection of lenses, as close as the tolerance of the birds permits. It is sometimes surprising how near a blind can be without disturbing the birds once they have grown accustomed to it.

Converted tent blind set up in the high desert of central Oregon to photograph displaying male sage grouse. Early morning temperatures, when displaying occurs, often drop to zero. This relatively spacious blind provided room for thermos bottles of hot coffee, sleeping bags, and other necessary items.

Commercially made portable blind about three feet square and four feet high. It is large enough for one photographer and equipment.

Photograph made from blind in photo on page 116 (above). Male sage grouse, *Centrocercus urophasianus,* displaying. 400 mm. lens, Plus-X film, 1/125 sec., f11.

A job for experts—building a blind on metal scaffolding overlooking
an osprey's nest.

Shot from the blind shown in photo on page 118. Female osprey, *Pandion haliaetus,* feeding fish to one of her nearly grown chicks. 600 mm. lens, Tri-X film, 1/500 sec., f16.

No responsible wildlife photographer does anything that might be harmful in any way to his or her subjects. When nesting, especially, birds may become too excited by the blind and the photographer's presence. If it appears that they may neglect their eggs, injure the young, or abandon the nest altogether, he or she should immediately remove the blind and look for other, less nervous, subjects.

It may be necessary to start with the blind some distance away and gradually move it closer each day until it is where you want it. It helps, then, to set up a dummy camera for a couple of days (an empty bottle will do) to accustom the birds to the lens sticking out of the blind.

Some birds get suspicious if someone enters the blind and does not come out. It may be necessary for two people to come to the blind and have one leave. Birds are not supposed to be able to count and are therefore satisfied that the blind is empty if one person walks away. This helper should return to the blind at the end of the photographic session and walk back with the photographer. (To have someone suddenly appear from the blind so close to the nest could well frighten the birds so badly that they would abandon it, but the approaching helper gives the birds plenty of warning, so they will leave without being unduly frightened.) This procedure is not necessary where blinds are set up at feeding areas or waterholes, where different individuals are continuously coming and going.

Most blinds are set up at ground level. Higher nests require complicated scaffolding or blind construction in a convenient nearby tree. Photography in this kind of situation is no different from that in any other blind. Only the construction is complicated and is not really recommended for beginners.

The best time to erect a blind is after incubation is well along. Parent birds are not so ready to leave the nest as hatching time nears.

Some birds are well feathered with down when hatched. They are active and able to feed themselves almost at once. These birds are called *precocial* and may leave the nest within a matter of hours. When photographing them, be alert for any indication of hatching so you can stay in the blind and get good coverage during the short period when parents and young are together in the nest.

Birds whose young hatch in a helpless condition, such as our American robin, are called *altricial*. These birds provide more opportunities for the photographer, since the young spend many days in the nest as they develop from naked, blind, and helpless babies into flight-capable juveniles. Pictures can be made of parents on the nest; hungry youngsters waiting with open mouths; parents feeding young, et cetera.

Nests may be partially or completely hidden by grass, leaves, or tree limbs, and the photographer may have to do a little "housekeeping" in order to photograph the nest. (When a photographer approaches a blind, the birds normally leave well before his arrival and return after he has concealed himself for a while. While the birds are away and before the photographer first enters the blind, he can do his housekeeping, usually in only a minute or two.) Sometimes it is possible to remove some of this covering without endangering eggs or nestlings. It is better, however, to tie obstructions back out of the way, so they can be returned to their original position after the photography session. Florists' wire is inconspicuous and excellent for this purpose. This nest cover provides protection from a damaging hot sun or possible discovery by predators. Nests in the open or in holes require none of this housekeeping, but there may be unsightly materials about that should be removed.

Some nest locations require the use of artificial light. Electronic flash is more satisfactory for this than flashbulbs. It does not seem to bother the birds as do the heat and strong flash from the bulb. Also, you do not have to be continually replacing bulbs and disturbing the subjects. Two flash heads are better than one, but one performs well if placed above the camera so that there will be no distracting side shadows. Flashes can be mounted outside the blind and near the subject with a long cord connected to the synchro-connection on the camera.

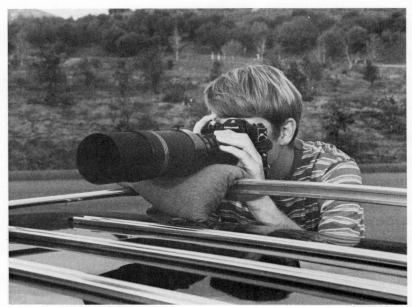

A beanbag is excellent for quick use and easily made. It can be filled with almost anything—sand, peas, peanuts, even beans.

Feeding killdeer, *Charadrius vociferus,* ignored the car from which this picture was made. 400 mm. lens, Tri-X film, 1/250 sec., f11.

I often photograph from my car and use a tripod arrangement that clamps on a lowered window glass. This provides a steady support if no one moves about in the car.

A small cloth bag, approximately 9 inches square and filled with dried beans or rice or some similar material is easy to use and most helpful in holding a telephoto lens motionless when draped over a car window. It can also be used outside on a rock, fence, or whatever is handy, and is an excellent substitute for a tripod.

It is important when using your car as a blind to keep movement and noise at a minimum. Animals seem to react especially to high-pitched metallic sounds. Some photographers carry huge camouflage nets and drape them over their cars for better concealment. I have parked my car ten or fifteen feet from such ground-nesting species as killdeer and avocet and had them show very little concern. They might scoot away a few feet but within moments are back on their nests.

Most of my car-blind photography involves driving slowly through areas where animals are present. When something is spotted, it is important to bring the vehicle to a slow stop exactly where you want it. Even very shy animals have some tolerance for cars. But if you travel too fast, come to a screeching halt in a cloud of dust, or overshoot and must back up, the subject will not stay around long enough for a picture.

Not all birds or mammals hold still for a car, however. You may make a half dozen stops before finding a cooperative subject. However, a lot of territory can be covered in this manner with a look at many potential subjects.

Killdeer, *Charadrius vociferus,* on nest, photographed with set camera. Camera fifteen feet from nest, controlled from inside house fifty feet away. 300 mm. lens, Plus-X film, 1/250 sec., f8.

124

It is sometimes possible to get good close-ups of birds or mammals with a "set" camera. In this instance, the shutter is operated either by some mechanical device or by the use of a long shutter release. I use a motor-driven camera powered by batteries. The shutter can be tripped by connecting wires from a distance. It is also possible to operate such a camera by radio, but I have not tried this method.

There are releases available of plastic or rubber tubing that are powered by a gust of air supplied from a hard squeeze on a rubber bulb or by a bicycle pump. They are strong enough to fire a shutter from as far away as thirty feet.

Here's how it works. A camera on a tripod is placed near a spot where your subject—squirrel, bird, or whatever—is expected to be. It should be focused on that spot, of course, and the area covered by the camera indicated by visible markers that won't show in the picture. You then wait, preferably hidden, as far away as your remote shutter release will permit. When your subject lands on the desired spot and the picture looks right, press the shutter release.

The drawback to this method is that the film must be advanced after every shot, unless, of course, you are using a motor-driven camera that automatically advances the film and cocks the shutter. It is, however, an effective method, though often time-consuming.

Birds and small mammals can be enticed to your marked spot if you place food there daily until they learn to expect it and return regularly.

Slow and careful stalking brought me within portrait range of this mature male pronghorn, *Antilocapra americana.* PHOTO BY LEON E. STUMPFF

By anticipating in which direction this thirsty male Rocky Mountain elk, *Cervus canadensis nelsoni,* would travel, I was in position for a photograph when it stopped for a drink. 300 mm. lens, Tri-X film, 1/500 sec., f11.

Although stalking is associated more with large mammals, it can be effective with larger birds too—particularly long-legged wader types such as herons and egrets. However, you can seldom get really close with this approach, and a 300 mm., 400 mm., or 500 mm. lens will be needed.

It has been my experience, whether stalking birds or mammals, that the approach is best made in full view of the subject while slowly moving in its general direction but never straight toward it. Avoid looking directly at the animal as much as possible. For some reason, animals seem to be aware of it when anyone stares at them. It makes them nervous and they may bolt.

Animals approached by a hidden stalker and surprised by his sudden appearance generally panic. The only picture one is likely to get is of a rear end disappearing in the distance.

I once spent most of four days practically living with fourteen mature bighorn rams on the National Bison Range in Montana. I used this approach on a roundabout route each day after I'd located the herd. I could get within forty feet, which was close enough for a full-frame shot of a whole animal with a 300 mm. lens. When I moved closer, they walked away. I was always forty feet away, their tolerance limit at that time.

I wanted to get nearer for portraits of their magnificent heads with full-curl horns, and I finally did on the fourth day. By then they had grown so accustomed to me that their tolerance limit was down to twenty or thirty feet. When they started to leave the feeding area, the apparent leader of the group ambled by me at about fifteen feet at a slow measured walk that produced a half dozen fine head shots.

127

I was being foolish here. Although this male black-tailed deer, *Odocoileus hemionus,* was raised as a pet, the approaching breeding season might have made it aggressive. A quick flip of those antlers could have done a lot of damage to my face.

A black bear cub, *Euarctos americanus,* is appealing, but photograph it from a distance. Don't get between it and its mother. 300 mm. lens, Tri-X film, 1/250 sec., f11.

In the field one should always be aware that there are some birds and mammals that are dangerous. Owls, hawks, and eagles may attack anyone or anything approaching their nests. A famous English wildlife photographer lost an eye to an owl who was defending her nest. Herons, egrets, cranes, and other large wading birds have sharp beaks that could seriously damage an eye. Normally, they are timid, but a wounded bird or one that for some reason cannot fly should be approached cautiously. It is best to leave it alone. If it needs rescuing, grab it first by the neck just below the head, but gently, so as not to injure it.

Swans and larger geese usually run or fly from danger. In some instances, such as in parks or reserves, where they have lost their fear of people, they may attack anything threatening their nests and render painful blows with wings and bills.

Any mammal in the wild that allows an abnormally close approach can be dangerous. It may be ill, hurt, or simply not afraid. Do not pick up or try to pet wild animals. As far as they are concerned, you are trying to hurt them, and they will protect themselves any way they can.

Park bears are not tame bears, and no one should hand feed or pet them, or otherwise try to be friendly. They don't understand "friendly." They understand food. If you feed one and then stop, it may pat you as a suggestion that you continue with the food. A bear's pat can tear off your arm. Besides, you can't get a decent picture of a bear that close. Let them wander off to the side of the road against some natural-looking scenery. Then they'll look like bears should, and you can get some good pictures.

There is not much chance of danger from smaller carnivores. They are mostly too shy. Raccoons are an exception in some parks, and the general rule applies: If they get too close, beware!

Squirrels and chipmunks are the mammals most likely to give you up-close photo opportunities. They won't hurt you if they come near. Just don't touch or try to pet them. Leave them alone and concentrate on getting a good, natural-looking picture.

The most dangerous times to be around mammals are during the mating season and while the young are with their parents. Possibly the most dangerous mammal in this country is a female moose with a week-old calf in tow.

Jim Straley of the Wyoming Game Commission has tagged many moose calves. But, he told me, he will not go near one unless there is a climbable tree nearby. On several unforgettable occasions, he and his fellow workers spent the better part of a day in a tree while an angry mother moose patrolled the ground below.

I have seen male moose, as well as male deer, elk, and bison attack—or threaten to attack—people that got too close. It isn't necessary to endanger yourself to get pictures, especially with the long telephoto you will undoubtedly have with you when photographing in the wild. A little thought, planning, and patience will usually get a good photograph for you safely.

7 Now that you have that telephoto lens you've waited for so long, you will want to head into the wilds at the first opportunity. *Don't do it!*

Spend a little time practicing with this new equipment—enough so that its use is easy and natural. This is a good rule to follow anytime you get a new camera or accessory or are trying different film.

I am never satisfied with a new camera or lens until I shoot at least thirty-six exposures with it and have them processed just to see that everything is working as it is supposed to. This also helps to familiarize me with new items. Fumbling around with a strange camera or unfamiliar film is almost a sure guarantee of missed pictures.

I have always found it best to shoot this test roll of unimportant subjects. This keeps it just a test and eliminates any worry about whether the photographs are usable. When trying new color film, I put together several objects with red, green, blue, and orange tones in bright sunlight ten feet or so from the camera. Then I shoot my photographs.

I wait for the processed film to be projected and evaluated before I use it on anything important. I am not concerned that it shows "true" color, but that it shows what looks like true color. Actually, the term "true color" is somewhat meaningless, I think. The color of any object is determined by the color of light reflected from it. What we tend to think of as true colors are colors as they appear on a normal, sunlit, blue-sky day between ten in the morning and about three in the afternoon.

I test black-and-white film and new lenses by shooting pictures of such things as signs, auto license plates, and printed matter on boxes, with the camera firmly on a tripod. The film is developed and enlarged (from 35 mm. negatives) up to at least 11" × 14". It isn't necessary, however, to make a print that size. An 8" × 10" or smaller glossy print can be made from part of the 11" × 14" projected image. Sharpness, or resolving power, of the lens is indicated by the sharpness of the printed image. The overall appearance indicates contrast and tonal values. If the negative appears normally exposed, the shutter and diaphragm can be assumed to be reasonably accurate and the exposure meter, whether built into the camera or separate, to read correctly. This isn't as scientific as it could be, but, from a practical standpoint, it works.

By this time, you should be impatient to try your photographic skills on some genuine wild "critters." But where can you go? There are a lot of good places, but it takes a while to locate and get to them. Many, though, are a lot closer than you think.

Some wildlife photographers are specialists and concentrate on waterfowl, songbirds, mammals, or insects.

Herring gull, *Larus argentatus,* photographed in Laurelhurst Park, Portland, Oregon. By waiting and being ready, this bill-open pose was
captured. 300 mm. lens, Tri-X film, 1/1,000 sec., f11.   133

Immature herring gull, *Larus argentatus,* taking a bath in Laurelhurst Park, Portland, Oregon. 300 mm. lens, Tri-X film, 1/1,000 sec., f11.

A trio of visiting western Canada geese, *Branta canadensis moffitti,* coming in for a landing on Mirror Pond, Bend, Oregon. 300 mm. lens, 134 gunstock-mounted camera, Tri-X film, 1/1,000 sec., f16.

I most certainly recommend that, in the beginning, you try your hand at any kind of bird or mammal that holds still for you. Insects need close-up (macro) work that calls for specialized equipment and techniques. Postpone them until later. Reptiles require some caution because a few are poisonous. They might well be left for a time when you have gained more experience. However, with caution and a telephoto lens, there is no reason to get dangerously close to any of them.

What you really want to find is a place where there are wildlife subjects that have lost enough of their fear of man to let you approach within suitable range of your telephoto lens.

State and National Wildlife Refuges, State and National Parks, National Monuments, local parks, and bird sanctuaries are all great hunting grounds for a wildlife photographer. But what you may need at the moment is something closer and easier to get to.

In Portland, Oregon, where I lived for some time, several of the city parks contain ponds that always have a population of resident waterfowl, sea gulls, and pigeons. During the winter months, the ponds are often crowded with northern ducks that stop to rest on their way south. The birds are fed by park visitors, and even the newcomers soon become accustomed to people. I have taken many quite satisfactory pictures there and in similar spots.

These might not be the wilderness locations your adventurous soul desires, but there is no appreciable difference between a wild duck in a Portland park or in your own home town, and one in the Canadian wilderness. So the first place to look is close to home. There may be more wildlife nearby than you realize.   135

Each spring in Drake Park, Bend, Oregon, free-flying resident western Canada geese, *Branta canadensis moffitti,* bring their broods in close.
136 100 mm. lens, Tri-X film, 1/500 sec., f16.

A female opossum, *Didelphia marsupialis,* that wandered into the backyard carrying her five young ones. 100 mm. lens, Tri-X film, 1/250 sec., f16.

A good rule to follow is never to pass up an opportunity simply because the location is not as wild and remote as you would like. With a little skill and the right viewpoint, backgrounds and foregrounds won't look much different from those in wild areas. 137

Female Roosevelt elk, *Cervus canadensis roosevelti,* with a thorn stuck in her tongue. A moment later she had it out. Prairie Creek State Park, northwestern California. 300 mm. lens, gunstock-mounted camera, Tri-X film, 1/500 sec., f11.

Two-month-old Roosevelt elk calves, *Cervus canadensis roosevelti,* playing in Prairie Creek State Park, northwestern California. 640 mm. lens, Tri-X film, 1/250 sec., f16.

Some seventy miles east of my home in southern California, there is a campground in the Anza Borrego State Park that is one of my favorite places for wildlife photography. Anza Borrego is harsh desert country and the campground, Agua Caliente (Spanish for "hot water") is located near a hot-water spring. I have spent many profitable hours there behind a long telephoto lens photographing desert cottontails, antelope ground squirrels, roadrunners, mourning and white-winged doves, California quail, white-crowned sparrows, and even an occasional coyote.

All but the coyotes are surprisingly unafraid. If I sit quietly in a lawn chair, ground squirrels and cottontails feed within a yard or so of my feet. Doves watch from nearby ocotillo so close that I can get full-frame shots of them.

I always carry with me several pounds of wild bird seed, along with a pound or two of raw peanuts. If there are no restrictions, I use modest amounts of these feeds to lure subjects within camera range. But there should never be seeds visible in the picture, and you should not use old, moldy, or contaminated food.

As you spend more and more time with wildlife, you will inevitably learn of places that provide good opportunities for wildlife photography. Many such spots you will discover for yourself, especially if you spend time reading about the subjects you want to photograph. You will also hear about them from other wildlife photographers, who, for the most part, are generous with their knowledge.

Male white-tailed deer, *Odocoileus virginianus,* in the spring after shedding antlers. Aransas National Wildlife Refuge, east Texas. 300 mm. lens, gunstock-mounted camera, Plus-X film, 1/500 sec., f11.

You can obtain information about state parks by writing to the State Parks Department and about State Wildlife Refuges by writing to the State Fish and Game Commission or State Department of Conservation, depending upon what they call themselves. Both will probably be located in your state capital.

There may be restrictions regarding visiting times to such areas, especially during nesting seasons. These should always be carefully observed, along with normal good wilderness manners. There is a saying about refuges, parks: "Take nothing but pictures. Leave nothing but footprints."

Usually little concern is shown toward those who only drive along the roads and take pictures from their cars. But if you want to wander around on foot or set up a blind, always get permission.

The U.S. Bureau of Sport Fisheries and Wildlife has divided the country into Alaska and six other regions. Addresses of Regional Headquarters are:

ALASKA AREA
U. S. Fish and Wildlife Service
813 D Street
Anchorage, Alaska 99501

REGION I
California, Hawaii, Idaho, Nevada, Oregon, Washington, Guam, American Samoa.
U. S. Fish and Wildlife Service
Lloyd 500 Building, Suite 1692
500 N. E. Multnomah Street
Portland, Oregon 97232

REGION II
Arizona, New Mexico, Oklahoma, Texas.
U. S. Fish and Wildlife Service
500 Gold Avenue, S. W.
P. O. Box 1306
Albuquerque, New Mexico 87103

REGION III
Illinois, Indiana, Michigan, Minnesota, Ohio, Wisconsin.
U. S. Fish and Wildlife Service
Federal Building, Fort Snelling
Twin Cities, Minnesota 55111

REGION IV
Alabama, Arkansas, Florida, Georgia, Kentucky, Louisiana, Mississippi, North Carolina, South Carolina, Tennessee.
U. S. Fish and Wildlife Service
17 Executive Park Drive, N. E.
P. O. Box 95067
Atlanta, Georgia 30347

REGION V
Connecticut, Delaware, Maine, Maryland, Massachusetts, New Hampshire, New Jersey, New York, Pennsylvania, Rhode Island, Vermont, Virginia, West Virginia.
U. S. Fish and Wildlife Service
One Gateway Center, Suite 700
Newton Corner, Maine 02158

REGION VI
Colorado, Iowa, Kansas, Missouri, Montana, Nebraska, North Dakota, South Dakota, Utah, Wyoming.
U. S. Fish and Wildlife Service
P. O. Box 25486, Denver Federal Center
Denver, Colorado 80225

For information about Federal Refuges in any state, write to the director of the region within which the state is located. He will supply you with a list that should give you the mailing addresses of all refuges in the region. A letter to the manager of the refuge in which you are interested usually brings information describing the 142 refuge and, almost always, a list of resident mammals and birds, along with migratory birds and their usual refuge visiting times.

If you want to ensure his cooperation for yourself and other photographers, remember also to write him *after* your visit. Let him know that you appreciate his help and advise him of your success or lack of it. It doesn't hurt, either, to send him an enlargement or two of anything you get that is especially good. He can always use pictures in displays and for visitor information. If you want to protect your photograph against unauthorized use, put your name on the back of the print and label it: NOT TO BE REPRODUCED WITHOUT PERMISSION.

National Parks can be approached in a similar manner. There aren't so many of them, and most highway maps show their names and locations. They are involved in things other than just wildlife—scenery and sports, for instance—so I normally write to the chief naturalist at the park headquarters for information about wildlife.

After you've accumulated some information about refuges and parks, you need to decide where and when to go. The *where* is easy. Pick a place you can get to that has the species you want to photograph. *When* should be based on the time of year that gives you the best opportunities for your chosen species. Unfortunately, summertime, vacation time for most school-age photographers, is probably the worst time for wildlife photography. That doesn't mean there are no good opportunities; just that there aren't as many as during the spring and fall. However, if that is the only time you have, go ahead. You may surprise yourself.

On a July trip to Tule Lake National Wildlife Refuge in northern California a few years ago, my grandson and

Female bison and calf, *Bison bison,* in May snowstorm. Yellowstone National Park. 300 mm. lens, gunstock-mounted camera, Tri-X film, 1/250 sec., f8.

I photographed mule deer, long-tailed weasel, western and eared grebe, killdeer, yellow-bellied marmot, golden-mantled ground squirrels, and many other animals.

Many of our wildlife refuges were established primarily for the protection of migratory waterfowl. Consequently, summer will find fairly empty those areas that are only stopovers during migration. However, protection of waterfowl means protection for other species. The refuge manager can tell you what animals are around and the best places to see them.

As mentioned before, early morning and late afternoon are activity periods for wildlife. Animals do most of their feeding at those times and therefore are most visible then. Obviously, this is the best time to find and photograph them. Still, I usually keep looking around even in the middle of the day. It is surprising how often something rewarding will turn up.

Several years ago, during a photographic safari to East Africa, our driver and guide always managed each day to be back at the safari lodge in time for lunch. They would not go out again until around three or four in the afternoon. Most of the tourists retired to their rooms after lunch and slept through the afternoon.

I hadn't traveled thousands of miles to take naps. I would grab a camera with a 300 mm. telephoto lens and prowl the grounds around the lodges. And although there were no lions lurking about for me to photograph, there were superb starlings, hoopoes, a dozen or so other bird species, and a rather ferocious-looking one-and-a-half-foot-long pink-and-purple reptile called an agamid lizard.

At Kilaguni in Tsavo West, my room balcony overlooked a waterhole that always had an elephant or two around it, along with a constantly changing group of animals such as antelope, gazelles, zebras, and wart hogs, regardless of the time of day.

You seldom see a professional wildlife photographer taking naps in the middle of the day. That might be just the time when the most unusual picture of the trip shows up.

One of the great things about wildlife photography— hunting with a camera, as some call it—is that there are no closed seasons. Nor are there many closed areas. All wildlife species are fair game, and there are no bag limits. Even better is the fact that no matter how many animals you "shoot," they are still there for you or someone else to "shoot" again. Your picture trophies are more meaningful than a dust-catching mounted head.

There are wildlife photography opportunities everywhere for the photographer who looks, thinks, and shoots. Don't wait for pictures of unusual subject matter —make unusual pictures of the ordinary. You have the tools and the knowledge. What you don't have is experience. You get that by taking pictures. So—why don't you get started?

Books for Further Reading

Bauer, Erwin A. *Hunting with a Camera: A World Guide to Wildlife Photography.* Tulsa, OK: Winchester Press, 1974.

Chandona, Walter. *How to Photograph Cats, Dogs and Other Animals.* New York: Crown, 1973.

Czaja, Paul Clement. *Writing With Light: A Simple Workshop in Photography.* Riverside, CT: The Chatham Press, 1973.

Hosking, Eric, and Gooders, John. *Wildlife Photography.* St. Lawrence, MA: Hutchinson, Merrimack Book Service, 1976.

Jacobs, Lou Jr. *You and Your Camera.* New York: Lothrop, Lee & Shepard, 1971.

Lahue, Kalton, ed. *Petersen's Big Book of Photography.* Los Angeles: Petersen Publishing Co., 1977.

Laycock, George. *The Complete Beginner's Guide to Photography.* Garden City, NY: Doubleday 1979.

Leen, Nina. *Taking Pictures.* New York: Avon/Camelot, 1980.

Noren, Catherine. *Photography: How to Improve Your Technique.* New York: Franklin Watts, 1973.

Richards, M. *Focalguide to Bird Photography.* New York: Focal Press, 1980.

Stagg, Mildred. *Animal and Pet Photography Simplified.* New York: Amphoto, 1975.

Sullivan, George. *Understanding Photography.* New York: Frederick Warne, 1972.

Sussman, Aaron. *The Amateur Photographer's Handbook.* 8th ed. New York: Thomas Y. Crowell, 1973.

Villiard, Paul. *Through the Seasons with a Camera.* Garden City, NY: Doubleday, 1970.

Weiss Harvey. *Lens and Shutter: An Introduction to Photography.* Reading, MA: Young Scott Books (A Division of Addison-Wesley), 1971.

INDEX

Italic page numbers refer to captions.

bobcats, *48, 75, 77*
brushes, camel's hair, 35
Bureau of Sport Fisheries and Wildlife, U.S., 141

cameras:
  care of, 35–36
  dust and, 35
  fixed-focus, 37
  holding of, *32,* 33
  110 film, 29–31, 33, 45, 69
  photographing through bars and fences with, 93
  point-and-shoot, 21–23, *22,* 37, 69, 87, 93
  range-finder, *30*
  "set," *124,* 125
  single-lens-reflex, *24,* 29, *104,* 105–107, 109–110, 111
  used, 31
  water and, 35
camouflage nets, 123
cars:
  animals' tolerance to, 123
  as blinds, 123
catadioptric lenses, 109
catchlight, *50,* 55
cats, domestic, 11, 75, *76,* 79
center of interest, *52,* 53, 69, 81
  light and, 69
  subject's eyes as, *50,* 55
chipmunks, 1, 3, 130
  Yellow Pine, *opposite page 1*
color, true, 132
common names of animals, 15
composition, 7, 39, 41, 47
  distance and, 41
  four points in, 53
  horizon line in, 53, *63*
  one-third division in, *52,* 53, 55
  see also backgrounds; foregrounds
contact sheets, 71–73

cottontails, 139
cougars, 75
coyotes, *18, 42, 74,* 75, 139
cranes, *51,* 129

deer, 15, *17,* 75, 130
  black-tailed, *128*
  Chinese, *92*
  mule, *42, 70,* 145
  white-tailed, *52,* 140
diaphragms, *see* iris diaphragms
distance, judging of, 41
dogs, 11, *74,* 75, 79
domestic animal photography, 75–82
  on farms, 79–82
  practicing with, 75
doves, 139

eagles, 129
East Africa, 145
ecological awareness, 3
egrets, 127, 129
elephants, 145–146
elks, *14,* 15, 79, 89, 130
  Rocky Mountain, *63, 126*
  Roosevelt, *6, 40, 68, 138*
enlargers, *22*
exposure meters, 27, 28, 37, 132
exposures, 33, 45, 69, 97
  correct, 25, 26, 37
eyes, subject's, *50,* 55

farm photography, 79–82
  large animals in, 79, 81
  small animals in, 79
feeders, bird, 114
film, 9, 23, 71
  black-and-white, 28, 39, 45, 132
  color, 28, 39, 45, 131
  fast, 27
  filters and, 39, 45
  heat and, 35

149

mallard hens, *80*
mammals, 11, *12,* 99, 135
  dangerous, 129–130
  mating season of, 130
  in refuges, 142–143
marmots, Yellow-bellied, *12, 54,*
  75, 145
Miles, Scott, *20*
monkeys, spot-nosed, *88*
moose, *8,* 15, 130
muntjacs, *92*

names, common vs. scientific, 15
National Bison Range, 127
National Monuments, 135
negatives, 71–73, 132
  care of, 36
  study of, 47
nests:
  artificial lighting and, 121
  blinds and, 115, 119–121
  photographer's "housekeep-
    ing" of, 121

okapis, 67
110 cameras, 29–31, 33, 45, 69
one-third division, *52,* 53, 55
opossums, *137*
orioles, hooded, 114
ospreys, *6, 119*
owls, 75, 129

parks:
  local, 135
  National, 135, 143
  State, 135, 141
perches, for birds, 114
photoelectric exposure meters,
  27, 28, 37
photographs:
  action in, 43, 81
  center of interest in, *52,* 53,
    55, 69, 81

photographs, *continued*
  composition in, 7, 39, 41, 47,
    52, 53, 55, 57, 63, 81, 87,
    93, *96,* 114–115, 137
  exceptional qualities in, 39
  framing technique in, 59
  identification as purpose of, 67
  improving of, 39, 47
  judging distance in, 41
  lighting in, 69, 81, 89, 97
  one-third division in, *52,* 53,
    55
  pictorial quality in, 37–39
  reason needed for taking of,
    61
  study of, 47
  technical excellence in, 37
pictorial quality, 37–39
pigeons, 79, *80,* 114
  crowned, *94*
point-and-shoot cameras, 21–
  23, *22,* 37, 69, 87, 93
prairie dogs, black-tailed, *30, 66*
precocial birds, 120
prints, 29–30, 36
  contact, 73
  study of, 9, 47
pronghorns, 75, 126

quail, California, 139

raccoons, *50,* 130
range-finder cameras, *30*
rangefinders, 23
reflections in glass, 93
reflective meters, 27
refuges, 145
  National, 135, 142–143
  State, 135, 141
reptiles, 11, *12,* 135
rhinoceroses, white, *20*
roadrunners, 139
robins, American, *112,* 120
roosters, leghorn, 75, *82*

151

wolves, gray, *34*

Yellowstone National Park, *opposite page 1,* 89

zebras, 146
Burchell's, *46*
zoological societies, 91
zoom lenses, 110–111
focal-length combinations in, 110–111

zoo photography, 85–100
backgrounds and foregrounds in, 87, 93, *96*
best times for, 89
difficulties in, 87, *90,* 91, 93–95
light in, 97
zoos:
animal behavior in, 99
animal feeding in, 99

ABOUT THE AUTHOR

JOE VAN WORMER is a wildlife photographer who has written and photographed many books about animals, including *Squirrels* and *Elephants,* an ALA Notable Book.

He says, "We lived near San Diego, California, for three years. During that period, I spent many pleasant and informative hours at the famous San Diego Zoo. I noticed that literally thousands of youngsters visited the zoo and that a surprisingly large number carried cameras. They obviously enjoyed the animals and wanted pictures, but it was apparent from watching them that most were going to be disappointed. They were making a lot of simple mistakes but ones guaranteed to spoil the picture.

"It seemed to me that a 'how-to' book on wildlife photography would be worthwhile. Forty-two years of photography, including twenty years specializing in wildlife, provided a good backlog of experience to draw on."

Mr. Van Wormer and his wife live in Portland, Oregon.